Günter Gerngross · Herbert Puchta

PLAYWAY 1

PUPIL'S BOOK

Unit 1 Hello 2	**Unit 8** Health 42
Unit 2 School 8	**Units 5–8** Show what you can do .. 46
Unit 3 Fruit 14	**Unit 9** Weather 47
Unit 4 Pets 20	**Unit 10** Food 52
Units 1–4 Show what you can do .. 27	**Unit 11** Animals 58
Unit 5 Toys 28	**Units 9–11** Show what you can do .. 62
Unit 6 Winter 33	**Extra Unit** Christmas 63
Unit 7 Party 38	**Extra Unit** Easter 64

Unit 1 Hello

1

❶ Watch the story. Listen and stick in the pictures (CD 1/2). Sing the song (CD 1/3–4).

2

Unit 1

○

○

1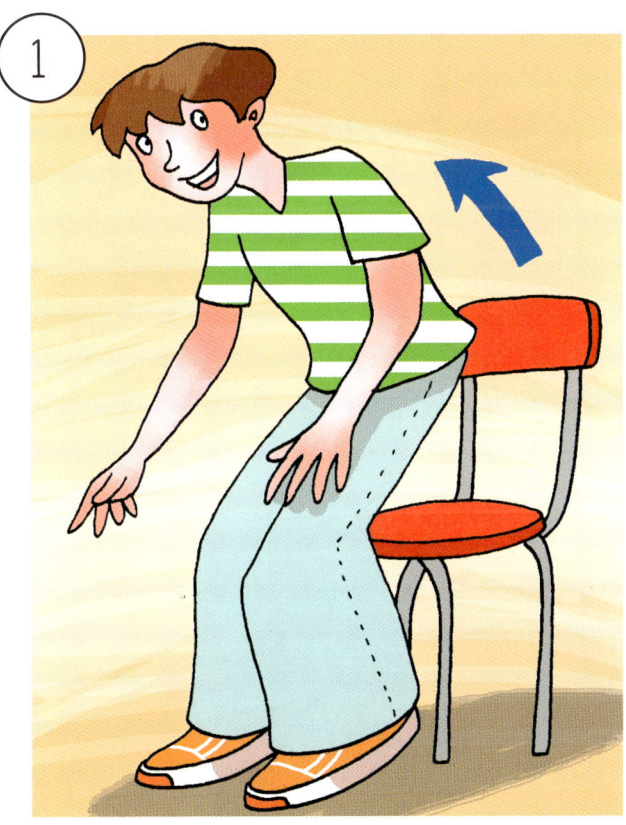

○

② Listen and point. Fill in the numbers (CD 1/5).

3

Unit 1

❸ Listen and point. Do the chant (CD 1/6–8).

④ Listen and point (CD 1/9). ⑤ Work in pairs. Look and speak.

Unit 1

 Listen and colour (CD 1/10–11). Speak.

7

🔴 Colour and speak.

Unit 2 School

1

① Listen and point. Do the chant (CD 1/12–14).

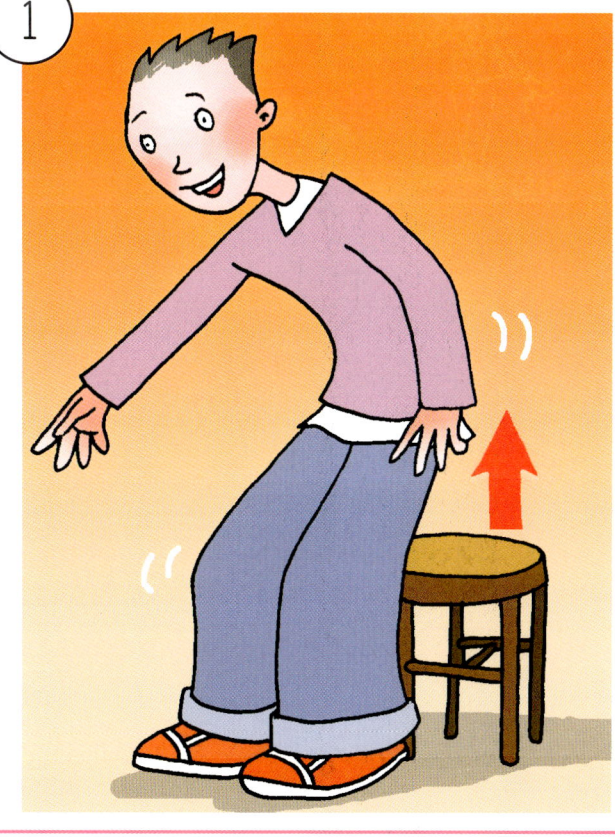

2 Listen and point. Fill in the numbers (CD 1/15).

Unit 2

 Colour and speak.

10

④ Listen and tick (CD 1/16). Speak ⑤ Stick in the pictures. Work in pairs. Speak.

Unit 2

6 Watch the story. Listen and stick in the pictures (CD 1/17).

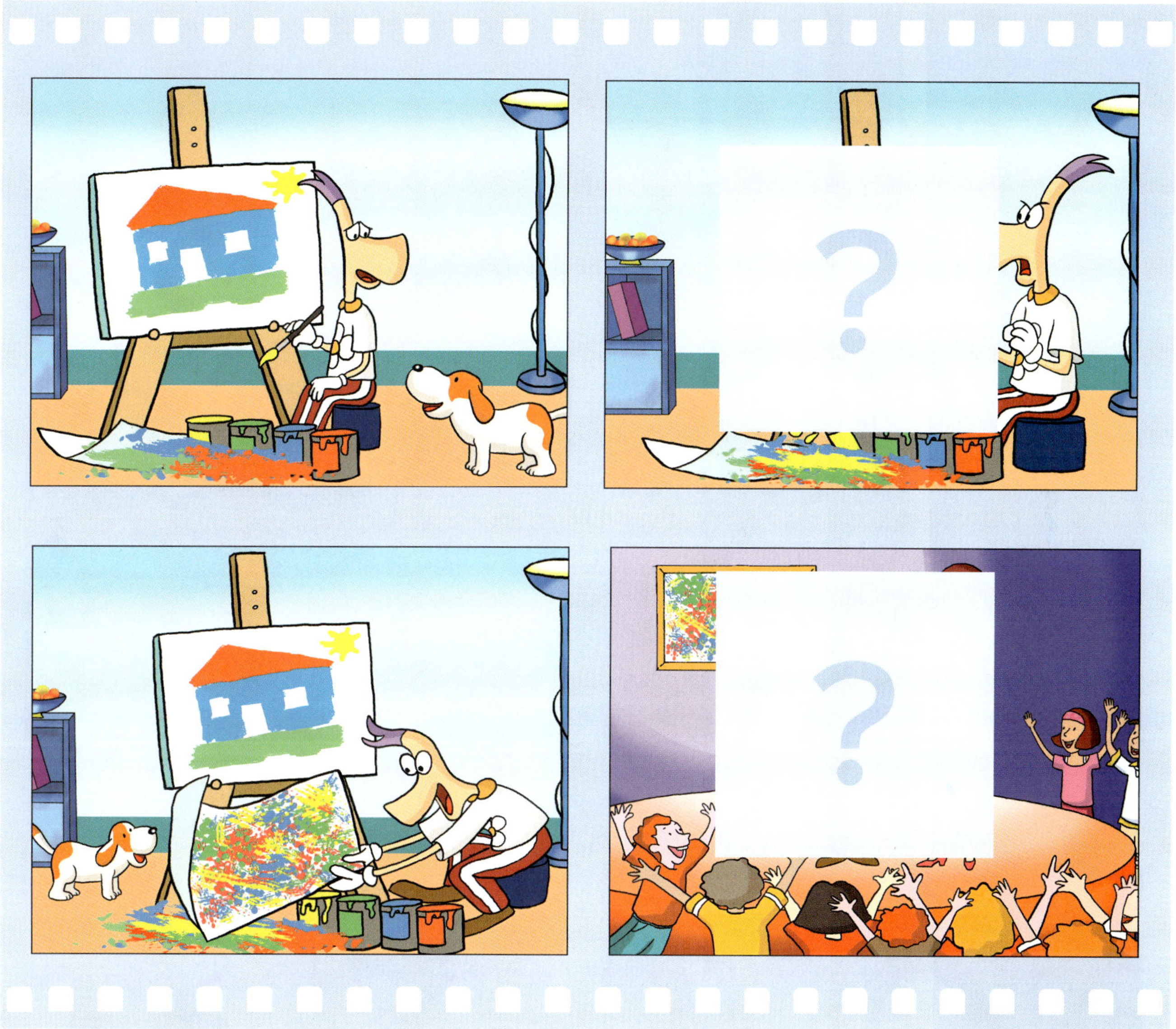

Unit 2

7 Work in pairs. Speak.

13

Unit 3 Fruit

1. Watch the story. Listen and fill in the numbers (CD 1/18). Sing the song (CD 1/19–20).

Unit 3

② Listen and point (CD 1/21). Work in pairs. ③ Think and draw.

15

Unit 3

④ Listen and point. Do the chant (CD 1/22–24).

5 Listen and point. Fill in the numbers (CD 1/25).

Unit 3

6

6 Watch the story. Listen and stick in the pictures (CD 1/26).

18

Unit 4 Pets

1 Listen and point (CD 1/27). Work in pairs. 2 Think and draw.

Unit 4

3 Listen and fill in the numbers. Do the chant (CD 1/28–30).

Unit 4

Watch the story. Listen and stick in the pictures (CD 1/31).

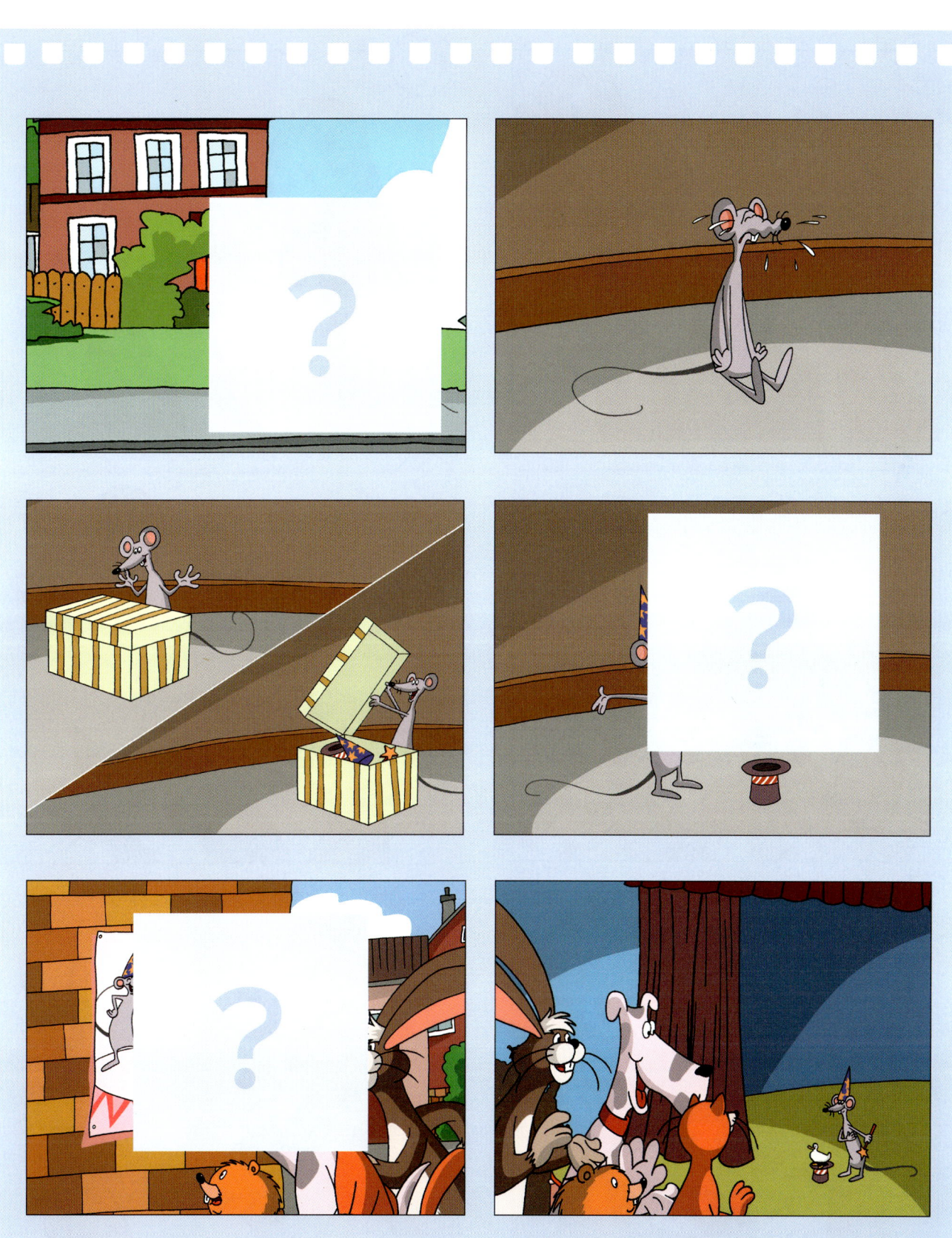

Unit 4

5 Listen and fill in the numbers (CD 1/32).

Unit 4

6

6 Look and colour. Listen and point (CD 1/33).

Unit 4

1.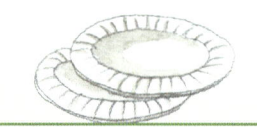

2.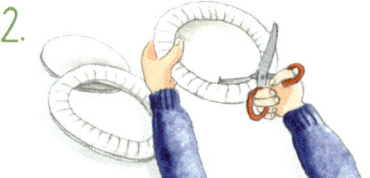

3.

4.

5.

6.

7.

8.

7 Work in pairs. Listen and point. Speak. **8** Make a fishbowl.

Show what you can do

Units 1-4

1

1

1 Listen, take a colour and number (CD 1/34). Colour and speak.

27

Unit 5 Toys

❶ Listen and colour (CD 1/35–36). Speak. ❷ Colour and speak.

3 Listen and point. Fill in the numbers (CD 1/37).

Unit 5

4 Listen and point. Sing the song (CD 1/38–39).

Unit 5

5

	 Anna	 Tom	 Lisa	
 🚗				
 ✈️				
 🚆				
 🧸				
 ⚽				

6

5 Listen and fill in the numbers (CD 1/40). Draw, fill in the numbers and speak. **6** Work in pairs. Speak.

31

Unit 5

7 Listen and point. Look and speak.

Winter

Unit 6

1

①

❶ Listen and point. Fill in the numbers (CD 1/41).

33

Unit 6

Listen and point. Sing the song (CD 1/42–43).

3

❸ Watch the story. Listen and stick in the pictures (CD 1/44).

35

Unit 6

4

5

④ Listen and point (CD 1/45–46). Speak. ⑤ Look and speak.

36

6

1.
2.
3.
4.
5.
6.
7.

Listen and point. Think and tick.

37

Unit 7 Party

 1

 2

1. Listen and point. Do the chant (CD 2/1–3). 2. Think and fill in the numbers.

3

❸ Look and colour. Listen and point (CD 2/4).

Unit 7

4 Listen and point. Fill in the numbers (CD 2/5).

❺ Listen and point. Sing the song (CD 2/6–7). ❻ Draw and speak.

Unit 8 Health

1

① Listen and point. Fill in the numbers (CD 2/8).

Unit **8**

② Listen and point. Sing the song (CD 2/9–10).

43

Unit 8

1

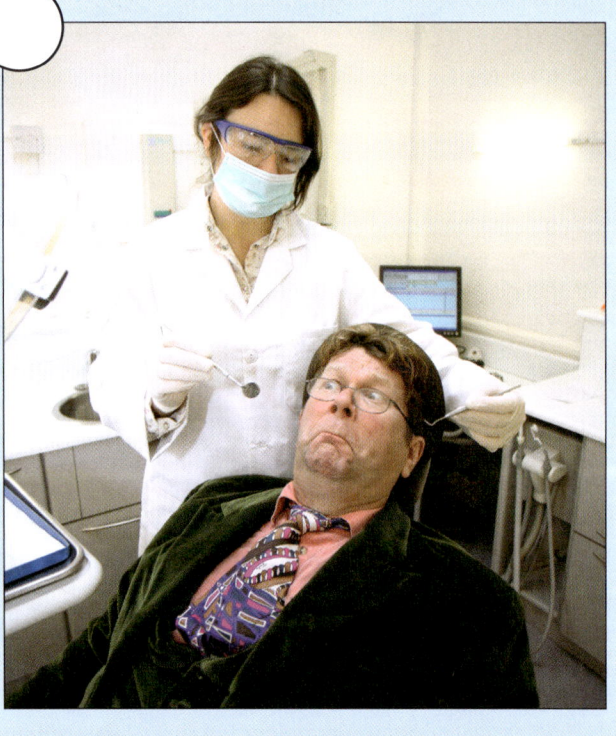

Watch the story. Listen and fill in the numbers (CD 2/11).

Listen and point (CD 2/12).

Units 5-8 — Show what you can do

1 Listen, take a colour and number (CD 2/13). Colour and speak.

Weather

❶ Listen and point (CD 2/14). Work in pairs. ❷ Listen and point. Do the chant (CD 2/15–17).

Watch the story. Listen and stick in the pictures (CD 2/18).

Unit 9

4 Listen and point. Sing the song (CD 2/19–20).

Unit 9

⑤ Listen and point. Fill in the numbers (CD 2/21). ⑥ Look and draw. Speak.

1.
2.
3.
4.
5.

7 Listen and point. Think and draw.

Unit 10 Food

❶

❶ Listen and point. Do the chant (CD 2/22–24).

Unit 10

2

2 Draw and speak.

53

Unit 10

❸ Listen and draw (CD 2/25). Speak.

Unit 10

④ Watch the story. Listen and fill in the numbers (CD 2/26).

55

Unit 10

5 Listen and point. Do the chant (CD 2/27–29).

Unit 10

1

6 Listen and point. Fill in the numbers (CD 2/30).

57

Unit 11 Animals

❶ Watch the story. Listen and stick in the pictures (CD 2/31).

Unit 11

Unit 11

❷ Listen and point. Sing the song (CD 2/32–33).

3

❸ Watch the story. Listen and fill in the numbers (CD 2/34).

Units 9-11

Show what you can do

1

1 Listen, take a colour and number (CD 2/35). Colour and speak.

Christmas

1

❶ Watch the story. Listen and stick in the pictures (CD 2/36).

63

Easter

1. Listen and point. Do the chant (CD 2/39–41).

Unit 1
Hello

Unit 2
School

Unit 3
Fruit

Unit 4
Pets

Unit 6
Winter

Unit 9 **Weather**

Unit 11 **Animals**

Extra Unit **Christmas**